AGING WEL

SAGE OR CURMUDGEON

PETER MENCONI

MT. SAGE PUBLISHING

Mt. Sage Publishing
Centennial, CO 80122

TABLE OF CONTENTS

ABOUT THE CASA NETWORK

In 1983, three Southern California churches established the CASA Network ministry to serve their 50+ members through coopera-tive efforts. The first jointly sponsored one day event was called Jamboree (now Life Celebration). The response to this first event led to a three day retreat held at a Christian conference center. A committee representing various churches met the next year to dis-cover how to meet the growing needs of the Christian adult senior community and to discuss incorporating. They determined that the name of the new organization would be called CASA, Christian Association of Senior Adults.

In 1993 the CASA Board of Directors caught the vision to broaden its ministry to mid and post career age men and women nationally and internationally. In the fall of 1994, CASA launched two quarterly pub-lications – The Energizer for senior adults and Energizing Leaders for leaders of Adults 50+ in the local church. With the explosion of the Boomer generation, a third quarterly publication was launched in 2001 for this population, called Legacy Living. For a time, CASA engaged in a website partnership with Christianity Today.

From 1993 through 1998 regional leadership training conferences were offered to pastors and lay leaders of adult 50+ ministries in a number of states and Canada. In 1998, the first National Leadership Training Conference was held in Irvine, CA and brought together over 300 pastors and lay leaders from 26 states and Canada. A fur-ther development in the growth of CASA's ministry was the estab-lishment of a website **www.gocasa.org** that provides resources and information on 50+ ministry. Serving leaders across the country, the CASA Network offers regional, national, and international 50+ lead-ership conferences. You can access the CASA Network website at **www.gocasa.org** for the latest information on training offerings.

Today, the CASA Network is a premier training and equipping source for the Church's ministry to midlife and beyond age men and women. Augmented by internet and print media, the CASA Network brings together an array of leaders within the field of 50+ ministry to inspire and equip the Church for ministry to and through adults in life's second half. Only God knows how many lives have been touched, how many churches have been changed, how many leaders have been trained because of the vision and leadership of the CASA Network. Check us out at **www.gocasa.org** and welcome to the CASA Network Aging Well Bible Study Series.

BEFORE YOU BEGIN!
Instructions on how to get the most out of this book.

The primary purpose of this Bible study is to help you to take a closer look at your attitude about aging, how to reevaluate your attitude, and how to move toward becoming a sage for younger people.

This book contains six Bible study sessions on the topics of wisdom and becoming a sage that can be done individually or in a small group. The studies are written for people who have never studied the Bible, occasionally study the Bible, or often study the Bible. That is, virtually everyone interested in aging will benefit from these studies. Each session allows the Bible to speak to where you are and where God may want you to go.

While these studies can be done individually, they are primarily designed to be done in a small group setting. In fact, you will receive maximum benefit when the study is discussed in a group. The more diverse your group is in age and experience, the more you will learn from these studies.

SUGGESTIONS ON FORMING A GROUP

1. Form a group that has between eight and 15 members. Groups larger or smaller are generally less effective.

2. One person should be appointed as the group facilitator. The facilitator's primary role is to get everyone together at an appointed time and place. The facilitator also gets the study started and keeps it going without getting off track. After the initial meeting the facilitator role can rotate within the group.

3. At the first meeting have the group members introduce themselves to one another and have each person share his or her responses to the following questions:

a) Where were you born and raised?

b) Where were you and what were you doing at age 10? Age 18? Age 25?

c) What one person, place, or experience has had the greatest impact on your life and why?

4. Before starting the study group members should agree on the length and frequency of meeting times. Normally, each study should take about one hour. All group members should commit themselves to attending all group sessions, unless there are circumstances beyond their control.

5. Give time for the small group to gel. Don't expect everything to click in the first session or two.

Because the interaction in a small group can reach into personal areas, it is important that group members agree upon "ground rules."

SUGGESTED GROUND RULES FOR SMALL GROUP STUDY

1. Jesus said that "the Holy Spirit, whom the Father will send in my name, will teach you all things and will remind you of everything I said to you." With this in mind, each group session should open in prayer asking the Holy Spirit to teach and guide. (Not everyone needs to pray. If a person is uncomfortable praying in public, he or she should be given freedom to remain silent.)

2. No one or two persons should dominate the discussion time. All group members should have an equal opportunity to express their thoughts, feelings, and experiences.

3. Because people's experiences and perspectives vary, there will be ideas, thoughts, and feelings expressed which will be quite diverse. All members should respect one another's perspective.

4. Confidentiality on what is said in the study should be agreed upon by all group members.

5. If significant conflict arises between specific group members, they should make every effort to resolve this conflict apart from group time. That is, they should agree to meet together at another time to discuss their differences.

6. If the group ends in prayer, members should pray for one another.

SESSION 1 | AGING ATTITUDES

INTRODUCTION
Have one or more group members read the introduction aloud.

The Issue: What is your attitude toward aging and do you need to rethink it?

Attitudes toward aging vary widely in our society. While we see stories on TV and the internet of older people doing remarkable things, we still see stubborn, negative attitudes toward aging. Despite the fact that the population in the United States is getting older, a youth oriented culture still dominates. From the 1950's onward, there has been a focus on the lifestyles of the young in the media. When older adults are depicted, they are not usually represented in a favorable way.

Starting in the 1960s, with the breakup of more and more marriages and families, we saw a reduction in the number of extended families. Young people had less and less contact with their grandparents and other older adults. With the decreased contact between the generations, we saw more stereotyping of older adults and the elderly. Older adults were seen as chronically ill, slow moving and slow thinking, a financial burden, and in other negative ways. These stereotypes are the basis of ageism. Ageism is defined as "prejudice or discrimination against a particular age group, especially the elderly." While older adults are usually the target of ageism, no age group is immune. We see older adults stereotyping younger people, and vice versa. Our attitudes toward youth, middle age, and old age often keep us from communicating and relating across the generations.

It is unfortunate that too many older adults have bought into the stereotypes associated with aging. When older adults believe that it is time to slow down and get out of the game, they may withdraw from younger people and relate primarily to people like themselves. For many older adults who have been active and productive up to this time, slowing down and withdrawing can have negative consequences. Many studies have shown that when older adults, especially retirees, stay active, they stay physically and mentally healthier.

Fortunately, many members of the Boomer generation are refusing to accept the stereotypes of aging. Pushing back on these stereotypic attitudes is important and healthy. Recent studies have found that our attitudes toward aging will be a powerful indicator of how well we age. For example, a study conducted by Yale University and the National Institute on Aging looked at surveys taken by 386 men and women in 1968, when they were under age 50. The researchers then studied the subsequent health records of the subjects. Nearly four decades later, the subjects who had held the most negative stereotypes about older people were significantly more likely to have had heart attacks or strokes than those who held more positive views. While researchers can only speculate on what causes the differences in aging outcome, it is clear that our attitudes toward aging directly affect our aging outcome.

In short, our attitudes toward aging are important. They can cause us to slow down and withdraw prematurely or they can keep us in the game as major contributors. For Christians, there really isn't a choice. Like many biblical characters, we are called to serve Jesus Christ until he calls us home.

YOUR TAKE
Read and respond to the following questions. Discuss your responses with your group.

1. Which one of the following statements best expresses your attitude toward aging?

___ I can't do anything about aging, so why try.

___ I greatly dislike the fact that I am getting older.

___ I am finding older age to be very enjoyable.

___ I refuse to accept the fact that I am getting older.

___ I have never been happier than I am now.

___ If it wasn't for all the aches and pains, I'd be OK with aging.

___ Financial burdens are making aging quite difficult.

___ Aging is only about numbers; I feel much younger than my age.

___ I just take life one day at a time and don't pay attention to my age.

___ Other _____.

2. From where have you derived your attitudes toward aging and the elderly? Have you developed positive or negative attitudes toward older people? Explain your responses.

YOUR REFLECTION

Read the following passages from the Bible and answer the questions that follow.

You, however, must teach what is appropriate to sound doctrine. Teach the older men to be temperate, worthy of respect, self-controlled, and sound in faith, in love and in endurance. Likewise, teach the older women to be reverent in the way they live, not to be slanderers or addicted to much wine, but to teach what is good.
—Titus 2:1-3

1. What is the attitude of Titus toward older people?

2. From these verses, does God expect older adults to get out of the game? If not, what are they called to do?

3. What do you think the term "worthy of respect" means? What relevance does the word "endurance" have for us as we age?

Therefore everyone who hears these words of mine and puts them into practice is like a wise man who built his house on the rock. The rain came down, the streams rose, and the winds blew and beat against that house; yet it did not fall, because it had its foundation on the rock. But everyone who hears these words of mine and does not put them into practice is like a foolish man who built his house on sand. The rain came down, the streams rose, and the winds blew and beat against that house, and it fell with a great crash.

When Jesus had finished saying these things, the crowds were amazed at his teaching, because he taught as one who had authority, and not as their teachers of the law.
—Matthew 7: 24-29

4. What is the rock upon which the wise man built his house? What foundation is Jesus asking us to build?

5. If we build a solid foundation on the teachings of the Bible, what would be our attitude toward aging?

6. What role does your faith play in the development of your attitudes toward aging?

YOUR APPLICATION
During the coming week think about the following questions.

1. What are your attitudes toward aging? Are your attitudes toward aging healthy or unhealthy?

2. What is the foundation upon which you build your attitudes and perspectives? Is your faith in Jesus Christ relevant to how you are aging?

3. As you assess the foundation upon which your life is built, are any changes needed? If so, what changes do you need to make?

SESSION 2 | ATTITUDE ADJUSTMENT

INTRODUCTION
Have one or more group members read the introduction aloud.

The Issue: As we age, we have the choice to become either sages or curmudgeons. Which way will you move?

In the last study we addressed the various attitudes toward aging that are present in our society. Certainly, it is important for older adults to think through and decide what kind of person we want to be for the remainder of our lives. As we age, we have a choice of whether we will be a sage or a curmudgeon. A sage is a person who is wise through reflection and experience. By contrast, a curmudgeon is defined as an ill-tempered, cantankerous old person.

All of us know a curmudgeon; the person who acts a lot like Oscar the Grouch, Eeyore, or Mr. Magoo. Curmudgeons often are grumpy and grouchy complainers who think that the world is going to Hell in a hand basket. Think of the Jack Lemmon and Walter Matthau characters in the movie *Grumpy Old Men*. Media has actually given us a long list of aging curmudgeons: Granny Moses of the *Beverly Hillbillies*, Andy Rooney of *60 Minutes*, Grampa Abe Simpson of *The Simpsons*, Archie Bunker, Fred and Ethel Mertz, and many more. Often curmudgeons complain that what ought to happen is for things to be the way they used to be.

For followers of Jesus Christ, a curmudgeonly attitude is not an option. Not only are we to rejoice in the Lord always, but we are also instructed to seek wisdom. For example, in Proverbs 4: 5-7 we read, "Get wisdom, get understanding; do not forget my words or turn away from them. Do not forsake wisdom, and she will protect you; love her, and she will watch over you. The beginning of wisdom is this: Get wisdom. Though it cost all you have, get understanding."

In this study, we will begin to see what the Bible says about the attitudes we should have as we age. We will see how the Bible contrasts the attitudes of the sage or wise person with the attitudes of the curmudgeon or fool. In some ancient and contemporary cultures wisdom was and is highly valued and actively sought. In our society we rarely talk about wisdom among our older adults. Yet, if there was ever a time when wisdom was needed, it is now. Today, older Christians have the opportunity to show the way on how biblical wisdom can be applied to a culture that is coming unraveled.

YOUR TAKE

Read and respond to each of the following questions. Discuss your responses with your group.

1. From the list of historical figures that follows, which persons do you see as wise or a sage and which do you see as a fool or curmudgeon. (Mark sages with an "s" and curmudgeons with a "c".) Discuss your responses with your group.

___ Winston Churchill   ___ King Solomon

___ Helen Keller   ___ Gandhi

___ Adolf Hitler   ___ Marie Antoinette

___ Martin Luther   ___ King David

___ Rosa Parks   ___ Saint Francis

___ Joseph Stalin   ___ Joan of Arc

___ Thomas Jefferson   ___ Albert Einstein

___ Napoleon Bonaparte   ___ Moses

___ Abraham Lincoln   ___ Margaret Thatcher

2. From the following list of characteristics, which are descriptive of a sage and which are descriptive of a curmudgeon? (Use "s" for sage and "c" for curmudgeon)

___ sensible   ___ disagreeable   ___ foolish

___ thoughtless   ___ prudent   ___ irrational

___ stubborn   ___ cantankerous   ___ shrewd

__ surly   __ ill-tempered   __ smart
__ judicious   __ astute   __ grumpy

YOUR REFLECTION

Read the following passages from the Bible and answer the questions that follow.

The wise in heart accept commands, but a chattering fool comes to ruin.
—Proverbs 10:8

A fool finds pleasure in wicked schemes, but a person of understanding delights in wisdom.
—Proverbs 10:23

The wise fear the LORD and shun evil, but a fool is hotheaded and yet feels secure.
—Proverbs 14:16

Those who trust in themselves are fools, but those who walk in wisdom are kept safe.
—Proverbs 28:26

If a wise person goes to court with a fool, the fool rages and scoffs, and there is no peace.
—Proverbs 29:9

1. From these Proverbs, how would you describe a wise person? How would you describe a fool?

2. How does a wise person's relationship with God differ from a fool's relationship with God?

For the message of the cross is foolishness to those who are perishing, but to us who are being saved it is the power of God. For it is written:

"I will destroy the wisdom of the wise;
the intelligence of the intelligent I will frustrate."

Where is the wise person? Where is the teacher of the law? Where is the philosopher of this age? Has not God made foolish the wisdom of the world? For since in the wisdom of God the world through its wisdom did not know him, God was pleased through the foolishness of what was preached to save those who believe. Jews demand signs and Greeks look for wisdom, but we preach Christ crucified: a stumbling block to Jews and foolishness to Gentiles, but to those whom God has called, both Jews and Greeks, Christ the power of God and the wisdom of God. For the foolishness of God is wiser than human wisdom, and the weakness of God is stronger than human strength.

Brothers and sisters, think of what you were when you were called. Not many of you were wise by human standards; not many were influential; not many were of noble birth. But God chose the foolish things of the world to shame the wise; God chose the weak things of the world to shame the strong. God chose the lowly things of this world and the despised things—and the things that are not—to nullify the things that are, so that no one may boast before him. It is because of him that you are in Christ Jesus, who has become for us wisdom from God—that is, our righteousness, holiness and redemption. Therefore, as it is written: "Let the one who boasts boast in the Lord."
—1 Corinthians 1:18-31

3. In these verses, is the apostle Paul suggesting that wisdom is bad? Why does scripture say that God will destroy the wisdom of the wise?

4. How would you contrast the wisdom of the world with the wisdom that comes from God?

5. When Paul writes about God's use of the weak and foolish things of the world to fulfill his purposes, what does this mean?

6. What role does a relationship with Jesus Christ play in obtaining true wisdom?

YOUR APPLICATION

During the coming week think about, answer, and act on the following questions.

1. If you are honest with yourself, are you more of a curmudgeon or a sage? As you age, which do you desire to be?

2. Do you desire wisdom? If so, what steps can you take to acquire greater wisdom?

SESSION 3 | WISDOM IN THE BIBLE

INTRODUCTION
Have one or more group members read the introduction aloud.

The Issue: What does the Bible say about wisdom and of what relevance are these teachings to our lives?

The Bible has much to say about wisdom, but much of the teaching is being ignored by Christians. There are several reasons for this lack of attention. Firstly, pastors rarely preach on wisdom. The wisdom taught in the Bible often demands something of us. Today, many churches want their congregations to feel good and comfortable, not stressed and stretched. Secondly, wisdom is not highly valued in our society and rarely talked about. Instead, our media highlights the dysfunctional lifestyles of the rich and famous.

Today, wisdom is in short supply. Look around. By most accounts, the world is a mess. Governments around the world are in upheaval. Economic ups and downs make the future look uncertain. Interpersonal relationships make great fodder for country music songwriters. Yet, we resist turning to the age-old wisdom of the Bible that is as relevant today as it was when it was written.

Wisdom in the Bible is not given to us to be pithy bumper sticker adages or "Confucius says" type insights. It is given to us for the purpose of helping us live righteously. All of us need guidance, but we don't always accept it. God, through his words of wisdom, wants to guide us to the best life possible, a life that will continue into eternity.

Following God's wisdom is not necessarily easy. In fact, it often put us in places and doing things that are counter to the norms of our culture and society. Sound familiar? Jesus Christ lived a life that went against the cultural current of his world. Yes, by human standards it cost him much, but he understood that he was doing the will of his Father. God, through his imparted wisdom, expects the same of us.

While wise teachings are spread throughout the Bible, there are certain books that are designated as wisdom literature. Traditionally, the books of Job, Psalm, Proverbs, Ecclesiastes, and Song of Solomon are usually thought of as the Wisdom Books. Like other examples of ancient Near East wisdom literature, these books focus on questions about God, humanity, Creation, and the nature of evil and suffering. Despite the march of secularism, these questions are still very relevant today.

This study will look at several examples of wisdom in scripture. As we look at these examples, we can ask ourselves several broader questions. Can the wisdom taught in the Bible help to make my life better? Is the guidance for living in the Bible better than guidance I am getting from other sources? Am I willing to look for creative and practical ways to apply the wisdom of the Bible to my life?

YOUR TAKE

Read and respond to each of the following questions. Discuss your responses with your group.

1. On a scale of 1 to 10, how important is wisdom and wise living to you? (1 = not at all important and 10 = all important) Discuss your response with your group.

1	2	3	4	5	6	7	8	9	10

2. Are there any verses or passages in the Bible that have provided you with insight and wisdom for living? If so, what are they? How did these verses or passages help you to live more wisely? Share your responses with your group.

YOUR REFLECTION
Read the following passages from the Bible and answer the questions that follow.

The fear of the LORD is the beginning of wisdom; all who follow his precepts have good understanding. To him belongs eternal praise.
—Psalm 111:10
The fear of the LORD is the beginning of knowledge, but fools despise wisdom and instruction.
—Proverbs 1:

The fear of the LORD is the beginning of wisdom, and knowledge of the Holy One is understanding.
—Proverbs 9:10

1. What does the phrase "the fear of the Lord" mean to you? Is there any relationship between fear and awe? If so, what is this relationship?

2. In what ways does wisdom begin when we fear God?

One of the teachers of the law came and heard them debating. Noticing that Jesus had given them a good answer, he asked him, "Of all the commandments, which is the most important?"

"The most important one," answered Jesus, "is this: 'Hear, O Israel: The Lord our God, the Lord is one. Love the Lord your God with all your heart and with all your soul and with all your mind and with all your

strength. 'The second is this: 'Love your neighbor as yourself.' There is no commandment greater than these."

"Well said, teacher," the man replied. "You are right in saying that God is one and there is no other but him. To love him with all your heart, with all your understanding and with all your strength, and to love your neighbor as yourself is more important than all burnt offerings and sacrifices."

When Jesus saw that he had answered wisely, he said to him, "You are not far from the kingdom of God." And from then on no one dared ask him any more questions.
—Mark 12:28-34

3. The Bible often contrasts the wisdom of humans with the wisdom of God. In this passage, do we see this contrast? If so, where and how do we see it?

4. Jesus was prepared to answer the questions asked of him. In what ways does biblical wisdom prepare us to answers the questions of life asked of us?

5. After Jesus answered their questions wisely, why did they stop asking him questions?

YOUR APPLICATION
During the coming week think about, answer, and act on the following questions.

1. What role or impact is wisdom currently having in your life? That is, has wise advice come to you that you have applied or need to apply?

2. Do you feel a need for greater wisdom in your life? If so, where can you go to find that wisdom?

3. Identify a wise person or two in your life. Schedule some time with them to ask questions and to glean some wisdom from them.

SESSION 4 | CALL TO WISDOM

INTRODUCTION
Have one or more group members read the introduction aloud.

The Issue: All Christians are called to be wise, so how will we answer that call?

The Old Testament chronicles Israel's struggles to understand and apply the truth and wisdom of God to their lives. As unique envoys of God's truth and wisdom, Israel left a mixed legacy. God gave Moses the Ten Commandments, wisdom which has helped to guide millions of people throughout the centuries. The wisdom and life of Solomon teaches us that wisdom alone will not save us from all foolishness. The wisdom books of the Bible (Job, Psalm, Proverbs, Ecclesiastes, and Song of Songs) give us practical guidance for many of the difficult issues we face in life.

Today, like with the Israelites, God calls his children. Yet, it is not always easy to hear and understand God's call on our lives. Often we are looking for some unique calling that puts us in our sweet spot. But for all of us who are called to follow Jesus Christ, there is a general call to wisdom. In Ephesians we read "be very careful, then, how you live—not as unwise but as wise, making the most of every opportunity, because the days are evil." Every age in human history has been an evil time, especially by God's standard. God has always wanted us, his children, to live out his wise agenda. Or as Paul goes on to write to the Ephesian believers "do not be foolish, but understand what God's will is."

As with them, our responsibility to God is to learn and apply his truth and wisdom. As we live out and apply God's truth and wisdom, we help to change and restore God's fallen creation closer to his original design. That is, we are called to wisely understand and apply God's truth in the world. By contrast, a "fool" is one who does not recognize God as creator and who, instead, chooses to live according to his or her human wisdom. Today, for most, this usually means making it up as you go along.

Ask most anybody, "who was the wisest person that ever lived?," and the majority of the time they will answer "Jesus." The wisdom of Jesus not only confounded the people who heard him, but his wise teachings often elude us today. Yet, we are without excuse. We understand what he meant when he said "Love the Lord your God with all your heart and with all your soul and with all your mind and with all your strength." and "Love your neighbor as yourself." We also understand what he meant when he said to his disciples "Why do you call me, 'Lord, Lord,' and do not do what I say?" Jesus calls us to live out his truth and wisdom. How will we respond?

YOUR TAKE
Read and respond to the following questions. Discuss your responses with your group.

1. Do you believe that you have received a call in your life? If so, what have you been called to do with you life?

2. Do you believe that a call to wisdom is only for a chosen few or for all followers of Christ? Please discuss your response with your group.

YOUR REFLECTION
Read the following passages from the Bible and answer the questions that follow.

Be very careful, then, how you live—not as unwise but as wise, making the most of every opportunity, because the days are evil. Therefore

do not be foolish, but understand what the Lord's will is.
—Ephesians 5:15-17

1. What is the relationship here between wisdom and evil?

2. In these verses, what is the relationship between wisdom and God's will?

I keep asking that the God of our Lord Jesus Christ, the glorious Father, may give you the Spirit of wisdom and revelation, so that you may know him better. I pray that the eyes of your heart may be enlightened in order that you may know the hope to which he has called you, the riches of his glorious inheritance in his holy people, and his incomparably great power for us who believe. That power is the same as the mighty strength he exerted when he raised Christ from the dead and seated him at his right hand in the heavenly realms, far above all rule and authority, power and dominion, and every name that is invoked, not only in the present age but also in the one to come.
—Ephesians 1:17-21

3. What role does the Holy Spirit play in providing us with wisdom?

4. What is the relationship between wisdom, hope, and power?

Consider it pure joy, my brothers and sisters, whenever you face tri-
als of many kinds, because you know that the testing of your faith
produces perseverance. Let perseverance finish its work so that you
may be mature and complete, not lacking anything. If any of you lacks
wisdom, you should ask God, who gives generously to all without find-
ing fault, and it will be given to you. But when you ask, you must be-
lieve and not doubt, because the one who doubts is like a wave of the
sea, blown and tossed by the wind. That person should not expect to
receive anything from the Lord. Such a person is double-minded and
unstable in all they do.
—James 1:2-8

5. Why should we be joyful when we confront trials and testing?
What does it take for us to become mature in our faith?

6. How do we obtain wisdom? What is the relationship between
faith and wisdom?

YOUR APPLICATION

During the coming week reflect and act on the following
exercises.

1. Spend several times this week in prayer asking God to reveal or
clarify his call on your life. When clarity comes, ask God in prayer
how he wants you to respond to his call.

2. Review the passages in this study. Reflect on how they might apply to your life.

SESSION 5 | APPLIED WISDOM

INTRODUCTION
Have one or more group members read the introduction aloud.

The Issue: How can we begin to more effectively apply biblical wisdom to our lives?

For Christians, wisdom is not to be experienced as a mountain top guru. We are not to resemble Gandalf as he imparts his wisdom to the Hobbits of Middle-earth. Or are wise Christians to go through life in a Yoda-like state quoting barely intelligible truths. No, the wisdom we receive from God is practical and relevant and can be readily applied to our lives and the lives of others.

The Bible is full of wisdom that can be effectively applied to every-day life. In fact, biblical wisdom usually gets right to the point: *A man who loves wisdom brings joy to his father, but a companion of prostitutes squanders his wealth. The wise in heart accept commands, but a chattering fool comes to ruin. Folly brings joy to one who has no sense, but whoever has understanding keeps a straight course. Evildoers do not understand what is right, but those who seek the Lord understand it fully.*

The application of wisdom is not based in judgment, but love. These verses from Proverbs remind us, *My son, do not despise the LORD's discipline, and do not resent his rebuke, because the LORD disciplines those he loves, as a father the son he delights in.* When we apply and impart God's wisdom, our motivation should be to lovingly share a great gift. When we pursue and practice God's wisdom, our lives change for the better and our influence on others seeks the best for them.

Perhaps the most important application of God's wisdom involves interpersonal relationships, that is, how we treat one another. Here's an example from the Bible:

This is My commandment, that you love one another, just as I have loved you. Be devoted to one another in brotherly love; give prefer-

ence to one another in honor. Be of the same mind toward one another; do not be haughty in mind, but associate with the lowly. Do not be wise in your own estimation. Owe nothing to anyone except to love one another; for he who loves his neighbor has fulfilled the law. Therefore let us not judge one another anymore, but rather determine this--not to put an obstacle or a stumbling block in a brother's way. So then we pursue the things which make for peace and the building up of one another. Therefore, accept one another, just as Christ also accepted us to the glory of God. For you were called to freedom, brethren; only do not turn your freedom into an opportunity for the flesh, but through love serve one another.

God does not force his wisdom and truth on us. We have a choice to either accept and apply his ways of wisdom and truth or make it up as we go along. When we choose to listen and respond to God, our lives and world are changed for the better. Especially, as older adults, God expects us to have a positive impact on the upcoming generations. God calls us to be sages who apply his wisdom and truth to a world that is broken and hurting.

YOUR TAKE
Read and respond to the following questions. Discuss your responses with your group.

1. As you were growing up, who in your life applied wisdom the best? Discuss your response with your group.

2. Which of the following statements best describe your feelings about applying wisdom to your life? Discuss your responses with your group.

___ I would apply wisdom to my life, if I knew what it was.

___ I have always tried to live as wisely as I can.

___ I have sought wisdom from God when I've had difficulties in life.

___ I don't need God to tell me how to live wisely.

___ I would like to reflect more and become wiser.

___ I would like to use my wisdom and experience to help younger people.

___ I have tried to apply wisdom to my life and it hasn't worked very well.

___ Other _____.

YOUR REFLECTION

Read the following passages from the Bible and answer the questions that follow.

So the Twelve gathered all the disciples together and said, "It would not be right for us to neglect the ministry of the word of God in order to wait on tables. Brothers and sisters, choose seven men from among you who are known to be full of the Spirit and wisdom. We will turn this responsibility over to them and will give our attention to prayer and the ministry of the word."
—Acts 6:2-4

1. From these verses can we deduce that the ministry of the word of God is more important than serving others by waiting on tables? Please explain your response.

2. Why would the seven chosen need to be full of the Spirit and wisdom?

Who is wise and understanding among you? Let them show it by their good life, by deeds done in the humility that comes from wisdom. But if you harbor bitter envy and selfish ambition in your hearts, do not boast about it or deny the truth. Such "wisdom" does not come down from heaven but is earthly, unspiritual, demonic. For where you have envy and selfish ambition, there you find disorder and every evil practice.

But the wisdom that comes from heaven is first of all pure; then peace-loving, considerate, submissive, full of mercy and good fruit, impartial and sincere. Peacemakers who sow in peace reap a harvest of righteousness.
—James 3: 13-18

3. According to these verses, how can we tell who has wisdom and who does not?

4. What are some of the differences between heavenly wisdom and earthly wisdom?

Instruct the wise and they will be wiser still; teach the righteous and they will add to their learning. The fear of the Lord is the beginning of wisdom, and knowledge of the Holy One is understanding. For through wisdom your days will be many, and years will be added to your life. If you are wise, your wisdom will reward you; if you are a mocker, you alone will suffer.
—Proverbs 9:9-12

5. In what ways does applied wisdom have practical consequences?

YOUR APPLICATION

During the coming week reflect and act on the following exercises.

1. Take some quiet time alone and reflect on what areas of your life can use some wisdom. That is, can you apply more wisdom to your friendships, work relationships, your marriage, your parenting or grand parenting, etc.?

2. Write down ways you can become wiser in the physical, intellectual, emotional and spiritual aspects of your life. Set up a regular schedule for you to apply these wise changes.

SESSION **6** | SAGE COACH

INTRODUCTION

Have one or more group members read the introduction aloud.

The Issue: Have one or more group members read the introduction aloud.

The Issue: As you age, you have a choice to make. You have an opportunity to become a sage coach who helps guide younger generations. Will you take advantage of this opportunity?

We live in very interesting and unique times. People are living longer, more generations are coexisting side by side than ever before, and technology is pushing life at a break neck speed. It is tempting for older adults to withdraw from the whirlwind of life. But our society and culture cannot afford to have older adults get out of the game, especially, when those older adults are followers of Jesus Christ.

In the previous studies we have seen that God has called his children to a life of wisdom. We can embrace this call or turn a deaf ear to it. We can seek to learn what God wants us to do with the remainder of our days or we can opt for a self-centered retirement. We can choose to proactively develop relationships with younger generations to help guide and influence them for Christ or we can avoid most contact with younger people because they annoy us. We can decide to use our God-given gifts, experiences, talents and resources to minister to others or we can keep all these treasures to ourselves.

Needless to say, our world needs sage coaches, older adults who are willing to share what they have learned. Many older Christians do not believe that they have much to offer. This is certainly not true. Our local churches and the greater kingdom of God are full of sages who are being underutilized. Often older adults are not given the opportunity to contribute what they have to offer. Ministry leaders need to call out the best our sages have to offer. If they cannot or will not engage older adults in kingdom ministry, older adults need to proactively find their sweet spot in the kingdom of God where they can use their gifts, talents, abilities, resources, and wisdom as God intends.

But how can an older adult become a sage coach? Here are some suggestions. First, as you age, you need to be willing to allow God to shape your later years. That is, you must continue to walk by faith and not by sight until your life is over. Second, in prayer, ask God what he wants you to do with the days you have left. Also, in conversations with like-minded believers begin to get a sense of your next step in your journey with Jesus. Allow other followers of Christ to speak into your life. Third, take that next step, even when the path is not totally clear. That is, when you have a sense of direction of what to do, move forward. Fourth, talk to a pastor or ministry leader who is involved in the type of ministry you have been directed to. Take advantage of opportunities to test out your skills as a sage coach with others.

How ever you move forward to become a sage coach, start using the wisdom of your years to help others. Together as older adults, let's start a sage coach movement that will positively affect God's kingdom for generations to come.

YOUR TAKE
Read and respond to the following questions. Discuss your responses with your group.

1. As you consider the others in your group, who do you think would make a good sage coach? (If you are doing this study alone, who in your life would make a good sage coach?) Spend some time in your group affirming each others gifts and abilities to be good sage coaches.

2. Does your church or community need a group of sage coaches to come along side younger people? If so, how might this group come into being?

YOUR REFLECTION
Read the following passages from the Bible and answer the questions that follow.

Therefore, I urge you, brothers and sisters, in view of God's mercy, to offer your bodies as a living sacrifice, holy and pleasing to God—this is your true and proper worship. Do not conform to the pattern of this world, but be transformed by the renewing of your mind. Then you will be able to test and approve what God's will is—his good, pleasing and perfect will.   -
—Romans 12: 1, 2

1. If we are not to be conformed to the pattern of this world, what is the alternative Paul presents to us here?

2. In what ways is the Christian life a countercultural lifestyle?

For by the grace given me I say to every one of you: Do not think of yourself more highly than you ought, but rather think of yourself with sober judgment, in accordance with the faith God has distributed to each of you. For just as each of us has one body with many members, and these members do not all have the same function, so in Christ

we, though many, form one body, and each member belongs to all the others. We have different gifts, according to the grace given to each of us. If your gift is prophesying, then prophesy in accordance with your faith; if it is serving, then serve; if it is teaching, then teach; if it is to encourage, then give encouragement; if it is giving, then give generously; if it is to lead, do it diligently; if it is to show mercy, do it cheerfully.
—Romans 12: 3-8

3. What should be our attitude as members of the body of Christ? How does this attitude relate to being a sage?

4. How are our God-given gifts to be used in the body of Christ? What is/are your gift/gifts and how are you using it/them?

Love must be sincere. Hate what is evil; cling to what is good. Be devoted to one another in love. Honor one another above yourselves. Never be lacking in zeal, but keep your spiritual fervor, serving the Lord. Be joyful in hope, patient in affliction, faithful in prayer. Share with the Lord's people who are in need. Practice hospitality.

Bless those who persecute you; bless and do not curse. Rejoice with those who rejoice; mourn with those who mourn. Live in harmony with one another. Do not be proud, but be willing to associate with people of low position. Do not be conceited.

Do not repay anyone evil for evil. Be careful to do what is right in the eyes of everyone. If it is possible, as far as it depends on you, live at peace with everyone. Do not take revenge, my dear friends, but leave room for God's wrath, for it is written: "It is mine to avenge; I will repay," says the Lord. On the contrary:

"If your enemy is hungry, feed him; if he is thirsty, give him something to drink. In doing this, you will heap burning coals on his head."

Do not be overcome by evil, but overcome evil with good.
—*Romans 12: 9-21*

5. These verses read like a lifestyle guide for Christian sages. Does God raise the bar too high for us to reach or do these verses help give us guidance in our journey with Jesus? Please discuss your response with your group.

6. As we age, in what practical ways does this Romans 12 chapter challenge us to be sages in the ways we relate to others?

YOUR APPLICATION
During this week reflect and act on these following exercises.

1. Check the following sage behaviors that you would like to make a part of your lifestyle. Sages coaches...

__ Educate themselves.

__ Are disciplined.

__ Admit their mistakes and learn from them.

__ Are patient.

__ Take instruction humbly.

___ Can handle rejection and failure.

___ Walk by faith and not by sight.

___ Know that they can only control themselves.

___ Are guided by wisdom.

___ Know their priorities.

___ Are trustworthy and steadfast.

___ Take calculated risks.

___ Make the most of their relationships.

___ Don't live beyond their means.

___ Don't squander money.

___ Respect and fear God and his word.

___ Listen and learn.

___ Value and control their words

___ Prepare for the future.

___ Associate with the wise.

2. Read Romans 12 every day this week. After reading, spend at least 5 minutes asking God to show you how to be a sage coach to other people, especially younger people. Pray that God will provide opportunities for you to have a positive impact on other for his sake. Make these prayers a part of your new sage coach lifestyle.

FURTHER READING

The Virtues of Aging by Jimmy Carter

30 Lessons for Living: Tried and True Advice from the Wisest Americans by Karl Pillemer, Ph.D.

Nearing Home: Life, Faith, and Finishing Well by Billy Graham

199 Treasures of Wisdom on Talking with God by Andrew Murray

The Practice of the Presence of God by Brother Lawrence

Wisdom and Wonder: Common Grace in Science and Art by Abraham Kuyper

ABOUT THE AUTHOR

Peter Menconi has written and presented widely on generational and aging issues. His rich background as a dentist, pastor, counselor, business owner, conference speaker, husband, father, and grandfather brings unique perspectives to his writing.

Born and raised in Chicago, Pete graduated from the University of Illinois, College of Dentistry and practiced dentistry for 23 years in private practice, in the U.S. Army and in a mission hospital in Kenya, East Africa. In addition, Pete has a M.S. in Counseling Psychology and several years of seminary training. He has also been a commodity futures floor trader, a speaker with the American Dental Association, and a broker of medical and dental practices.

For over 20 years Pete was the outreach pastor at a large church in suburban Denver, Colorado. Currently, he is the president of Mt. Sage Publishing and board member with the CASA Network.

Pete's writings include the book *The Intergenerational Church: Understanding Congregations from WWII to www.com*, The Support Group Series, a 9-book Bible study series, and numerous articles.

Pete and his wife Jean live in the Denver area and they are the parents of 3 adult children and the grandparents of 9 grandchildren.

Pete Menconi can be reached at petermenconi@msn.com.

CASA NETWORK

AGING WELL

BIBLESTUDY**SERIES**

Finally, a Bible study series for everyone 50 and over
who wants to stay in the game as long as possible!

THE AGING CHALLENGE

The primary purpose of this Bible study is to
help you take a fresh look at aging, reevaluate
your current situation, and consider making
some changes.

THE NEW R & R: RETIRED AND REWIRED

The primary purpose of this Bible study is to
help you to take a fresh look at retirement,
reevaluate your current situation, and consider
making some changes.

GENERATIONS TOGETHER

The primary purpose of this Bible study is to
help you to take a fresh look at our current
generations, how the generations relate, and
how we can be better together.

Available at www.Amazon.com

SAGE OR CURMUDGEON

The primary purpose of this Bible study is to help you to take a closer look at your attitude about aging, how to reevaluate your attitude, and how to move toward becoming a sage for younger people.

THE AGING FAMILY AND MARRIAGE

The primary purpose of this Bible study is to help you to take a closer look at your aging marriage and/or family and see how you can maximize these relationships.

FINISHING WELL

The primary purpose of this Bible study is to help you to take a closer look at how you can finish well before your life is over.

Available at www.Amazon.com

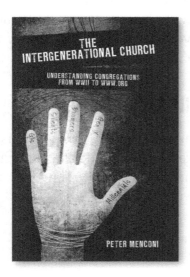

Made in the USA
Monee, IL
12 February 2025

12138236R00036